LOVE A
DUB DOVE

Cormac G. McDermott, BA, MEconSc

Order this book online at www.trafford.com
or email orders@trafford.com

Most Trafford titles are also available at major online book retailers.

Printed in the United States of America.

ISBN: 978-1-4907-4572-5 (sc)
ISBN: 978-1-4907-4571-8 (e)

Trafford rev. 10/01/2014

 www.trafford.com

North America & international
toll-free: 1 888 232 4444 (USA & Canada)
fax: 812 355 4082

Contents

Chapter 1

COMEDY SKETCHES

SCENE FROM A DUBLIN SUBURB—FIONA AND DOUG ARE
WALKING BY A SCHOOL.

FIONA: 'That's meant to be a really good school, Doug'.

DOUG: 'Oh, is that so?'

FIONA: 'Yeah. Children from all over the place come
            to it. It was voted the top inter-denominational
            primary school in Dublin'.

DOUG: 'Well. Maybe we should try get our kids in there,
            ey?'

FIONA: 'I'd love that'.

FIONA SPOTS SOMETHING GOING ON IN THE PLAYGROUND.

FIONA: 'Look at that big bully frightening the infants. If I
            was to get my hands on him'.

DOUG: 'Maybe he was bullied himself at some stage'.

FIONA: 'No. I recognise him. That's Jack D'arcy. He's a little b*llix'.

DOUG: 'One of the teachers seems to be sorting things out so don't get too worked up'.

FIONA: 'Mmm. He's giving him a bit of a ticking off. I'm telling ya, even if the fecker got a mosquito bite on his mickey, he'd still 'pick on' it'!

DOUG CHUCKLES.

SCENE FROM A SITTING ROOM—TWO PALS (JOHN AND MAXI)
ARE WATCHING A SPORTS NEWS CHANNEL.

VOICE FROM
THE TELLY: 'Riots have broken out in Rome today between rival fans after a big club game'.

JOHN: 'For goodness sake. That's disturbing footage, Maxi'.

MAXI: 'I know. It puzzles me that some people can't even go to a football match and refrain from causing trouble'.

JOHN: 'It's only a game. What on earth is wrong with these guys?'

MAXI: 'Look. The police are having to use water canons to displace them'.

JOHN: 'Fecking animals'.

MAXI: 'That's an insult to animals, John. God put animals on earth to help people and show humans what they can be like, He didn't put humans here to make animals look sophisticated'!

JOHN: 'Very good, Maxi. The muppets should take a good look at themselves from the outside alright'.

SCENE FROM A WORKING CLASS HOUSE—PHELIM AND NICOLE ARE HAVING A MEAL TOGETHER.

PHELIM: 'I heard on the radio earlier that the economy is expected to grow by three per cent next year'.

NICOLE: 'Thank God for that. It might mean the factory will give me more hours'.

PHELIM: 'Yeah, hopefully they will, love. At least we want to work unlike that wagon Lola LaDola from next door'.

NICOLE: 'I know. It would make you sick the way she just has babies and claims everything off the Government'.

PHELIM: 'Even if the jobs become available when things improve, I honestly don't think you'll find her out looking for work'.

NICOLE: 'Of course not. People of that ilk are just parasites'.

PHELIM: 'Lola LaDola me arse. Lola La Bleedin' DOLE-ITE more like it'!

THE COUPLE CHUCKLE.

SCENE FROM A LIVING ROOM IN THE UNITED STATES—CHAD AND JOSH ARE WATCHING A GAME OF COLLEGE GRIDIRON ON TELEVISION.

CHAD: 'This is a fairly bruising encounter, Josh'.

JOSH: 'Yeah, I know. There are some real big hits going in dude'.

CUT TO THE TELEVISION. A PLAY HAPPENS AND A HEAVY TACKLE HAS BEEN PUT ON A GUY WHO LOSES HIS HELMET IN THE PROCESS AND CLASHES HEADS WITH AN OPPONENT.

CHAD: 'Oh, Lord. Did you see that? That was rough, right?'

JOSH: 'It sure was. Look at the size of the lump which has come up on the forehead of that poor dude from The Fightin' Irish'.

CHAD: 'Aw, man. He's going to have one sore head tomorrow. What's his name?'

JOSH: 'He's a French dude called Jean Claude Modo'.

CHAD: 'Jean Claude Modo. With a lump that size, I bet he'll be referred to as The Hunch HEAD Of Notre Dame from now on, right?'!

JOSH BEGINS TO GIGGLE.

JOSH: 'Right, dude. You crack me up man'!

SCENE FROM AN INTERNET FORUM—BANTER IS FLOWING BETWEEN A COUPLE OF FOOTBALL FANS FROM RIVAL CLUBS.

CHEVVY: 'Looks like you lot have really messed up in the run-in mate'.

BART: 'Yeah, I know. At least we gave it a right good go this season though'.

CHEVVY: 'It's been a few campaigns since you last did that, ey?'

BART: 'True. It's disappointing but at least we were made to dream'.

CHEVVY: 'Not like us. We were out of the running before Christmas'.

BART: 'Well, I have to say I can empathise with that buddy'.

CHEVVY: 'There's always next season'.

BART: 'I'm going to try stay optimistic that our coach will continue to keep us going forward'.

CHEVVY: 'From my viewpoint, I hope we improve dramatically. Our home ground is no longer a fortress'.

BART: 'Indeed. You got so many 'beatings at home', you'd swear your manager was your father who's an aggressive, sexually repressed and mentally unstable war vet who took to consuming excessive amounts of alcohol'!

CHEVVY: 'Goodness me! You've a point there! H'har har'!

SCENE FROM A LIVING ROOM—GRAHAM AND ERIC ARE CHATTING AWAY.

GRAHAM: 'I'm feeling a bit peckish. I think I'll order a Chinese. Would you like anything?'

ERIC: 'I only had my dinner before I came out but get us a bag of prawn crackers anyway mate, will ya?'

GRAHAM: 'No probs'.

GRAHAM LEAVES THE ROOM TO PHONE THE TAKE-AWAY AND RETURNS SEVERAL MINUTES LATER.

ERIC: 'What did you order for yourself?'

GRAHAM: 'Just the king prawn in hot garlic sauce with boiled rice'.

ERIC: 'Why boiled rice?'

GRAHAM: 'Ah, you spotted. I'm watching my cholesterol'.

ERIC: 'Good man. Fair play to you. Here, I'll give you the two euro for those prawn crackers'.

GRAHAM: 'Don't be silly pal. They're on me'.

ERIC: 'Cheers, Graham. I must say your house is looking well'.

GRAHAM: 'Thanks'.

THE DOOR BELL RINGS.

GRAHAM: 'Goodness me, that was quick'.

GRAHAM LEAVES THE ROOM AGAIN AND RETURNS A COUPLE OF MINUTES LATER LOOKING DISAPPOINTED.

ERIC: 'What's up? Where's your food?'

GRAHAM: 'It was a politician canvassing for the Local Elections'.

ERIC: 'Are you serious? What did you say to him?'

GRAHAM: 'I just told him I was busy and didn't have time to talk'.

ERIC: 'I wouldn't say too many people are interested in talking to them these days and, if they do, they probably just give them grief'.

GRAHAM: 'I know. These property and waters taxes have lots fuming'.

ERIC: 'Hey mate. What do you think of this?: 'BREAKING NEWS: Please be aware of the new term 'howissh*le' i.e. what people in Dublin should call the assh*le in Government who came up with the idea that there should be a tax on your gaff'!

GRAHAM: 'Bahahaha. Nice one, Eric. That's right. 'De HOWISSH*LE Tax. A tax on howissh*les made by howissh*les'!

BOTH LADS BREAK OUT IN A FIT.

SCENE FROM A STREET—BUZZ AND JAMMY ARE CHATTING.

BUZZ: 'Hiya, Jammy. Has your brown bin not been collected yet either mate?'

JAMMY: 'No it hasn't. I'm just back from the shops. There's some blokes from the local refuse collectors refusing to let a truck get by'.

BUZZ: 'Is that what the story is? I was wondering. Normally they are here by eight a.m.'.

JAMMY: 'I know. Apparently some of the labourers are out on strike because they are being asked to work for less pay'.

BUZZ: 'They are probably down there because they feel betrayed by their co-workers who they think have broken a picket line, ey?'

JAMMY: 'That's exactly what's going on alright'.

BUZZ: 'I tell ya, I sympathise with men who believe they can't be expected to survive on less income but it's becoming so frequent, it's getting a bit ridiculous, don't you think?'

JAMMY: 'Not at all. They deserve a decent standard of living too. If their bosses were asked to take a thirty five per cent pay cut when they are already struggling to survive, they'd be 'all out for next to nothing' more often than the Peruvian international cricket team aswell'!

BUZZ: 'Bahahaha. I suppose that's true alright'!

SCENE FROM A PARK—NICOLE AND PHELIM ARE HAVING A PICNIC DURING SUMMER.

NICOLE: 'Cover up the strawberries there, Phelim. They'll attract wasps'.

PHELIM: 'Yeah, no probs. Good idea'.

NICOLE: 'Did you put your sunscreen on?'

PHELIM: 'I sprayed some over my head and face earlier. Cheers for reminding me anyway'.

NICOLE: 'It's a blessing we are getting this good weather here at home given we couldn't afford a holiday abroad this year, ey?'

PHELIM: 'It is'.

NICOLE: 'Oh, this is The Script coming on the radio. I love them'.

PHELIM: 'What song of theirs' is it?'

NICOLE: 'The Man Who Can't Be Moved'.

PHELIM: 'Well, whoever wrote that song has obviously never seen the end of 'E.T.''!

SCENE FROM A FRONT DOOR—THE ELECTIONS ARE IMMINENT AND A POLITICIAN (BORIS) HAS CALLED TO A HOUSE.

BORIS: 'Hi there. I'm sure you are aware the Elections are coming up and I'll be looking for your vote. Have you any issues you'd like addressed?'

JEM: 'Oi dohne know whethaw oyim gowin' teh even voh argh awll. Oi've a bleedin' payin in me b*llix with you pawlitishins'! (I don't know whether I'm going to even vote at all. I've a bleeding pain in my scrotum with you politicians!).

BORIS: 'Well, what seems to be concerning you?'

JEM: 'De peepill who avteh gerrin' us inteh diss mess argh gerrin' away wirreh. Diss cuntree is awll for de rich'! (The people who have got us in to this mess are getting away with it. This country is all for the rich'!).

BORIS: 'We're working to get the economy up and running once again, sir'.

JEM: 'I tink yiz argh awll a showaw eh lyers. De howisshole tax and now diss wawtawh charge have me reelee annoyid'! (I think you are all a shower of liars. The household tax and now this water charge have me really annoyed!).

BORIS: 'My party are looking to release funds to help education and improve the standard of living of the needy'.

JEM: 'Lissin, yiz awll say dah burrazz sooin as yiz gerrin tih powaw, yiz break awll of yizzaw prawmississ. I dohn wawhn tih talk faw much longaw. Wotz yaw full nayim and oi myh consideraw yeh cum a Sahdeh when itz tyim tih voh'! (Listen, you all say that but as soon as you get in to power, you break all of your promises. I don't want to talk for much longer. What's your full name and I might consider you come Saturday when it's time to vote!).

BORIS: 'I'm Boris Greenhoff'.

JEM: 'Well, ih sowinds lykh yorrah Russian who myh be good faw dee envoyardinmint anyway! Alryh, tanx faw cawllin'! (Well, it sounds like you are a Russian who might be good for the environment anyway! Alright, thanks for calling!).

BORIS HANDS JEM A LEAFLET AND WALKS AWAY.

SCENE FROM A HOUSE. NICOLE AND PHELIM ARE LISTENING TO A RADIO STATION STUDIO—MARIA IS HOSTING A RELIGIOUS SHOW.

MARIA: 'Hi. Welcome along to The God Show. With me this evening I have Gavin Kelly who lectures in systematic theology at the Holy Faithful College, Drumcondra here in Dublin and along with him my guest is Phillip McCabe who is a professor in religious studies at the Christ The Redeemer College, Terenure here in Dublin also. Great to have you two gentlemen in the studio'.

GAVIN: 'Nice to be here, Maria'.

PHILLIP: 'Thank you for inviting me here tonight'.

MARIA: 'The topic up for discussion is going to be the relevance of the Papacy in modern day Ireland. If I could start with you, Gavin'.

GAVIN: 'Firstly, may I say that I think a lot of people need to fill a spiritual void in their lives. Most are being caught up in world affairs and I feel they should be looking for 'faith enhancing nourishment' from religious leaders'.

MARIA: 'How about you, Phillip?'

PHILLIP: 'I agree with Gavin. A lot of individuals are saying that the Bible in particular is no longer relevant to modern living but those who are aware of the fact that we are about to enter a very troubling time period know that understanding the truth is more vital than it's ever been'.

MARIA: 'I see'.

GAVIN: 'Roman Catholics have always looked to the Pope for guidance and, although the various Vatican leaders have had profound things to say throughout the centuries, it's time we re-established Jesus Christ in our belief system'.

PHILLIP: 'I must say I am in agreement with Mr. Kelly again. My own personal viewpoint is that when the Lord said to Peter 'thou art Peter and upon this rock I build my Church', He was letting Peter and those listening know that it was the teaching which he gave during His public ministry which is the rock'.

MARIA: 'That's very interesting. Would either of you like to add to what you have said?'

GAVIN: 'Mr. McCabe is right. The rock on which the church is built is Jesus Christ's teaching. If Peter and every Pope who has existed was a rock, how many rocks would the Church be built on?'

PHILLIP: 'He's right. There is only one rock and that's our Saviour's ministry. All He did was quote Old Testament and speak in the parables Yahweh educated Him to. If people focus too much of their attention on the Pope, then what the Lord taught might be diluted or even forgotten about'.

GAVIN: 'Yes. Just because the New Testament involves Jesus, we as Christians, should not discard the Old one because Christ was basically an Old Testament fundamentalist. What we must accept is the Old Testament, the New and by faith believe St. Paul was divinely inspired to write what he did also'.

MARIA: 'So what you are both saying is that there is only one rock and that is Jesus Christ's teaching and accepting correct interpretation of Scripture is the way for people to feed themselves spiritually?'

PHILLIP: 'Absolutely. Jesus' ministry is the only rock and not all the Popes that followed. If they were, you'd have so many 'rocks' you could have armed all those Civil Rights demonstrators throughout Ulster during the Troubles and then built a pyramid the size of Kilimanjaro thereafter'!

ALL THREE MEMBERS OF THE DISCUSSION START TO LAUGH.

NICOLE AND PHELIM CHUCKLE TOO.

SCENE FROM A HARDWARE STORE—GRAHAM AND ERIC ARE
SHOPPING FOR SOME GOODS.

GRAHAM: 'What is it precisely you're looking for, Eric?'

ERIC: 'A multi-purpose work bench mate. I'm going to be wall-papering my bedroom soon and will need something to lay the wall-paper on to put paste on it'.

GRAHAM: 'Look over there. That might be what you require'.

ERIC LOOKS OVER.

ERIC: 'Yeah. It could do the trick alright'.

THEY WALK OVER.

ERIC: 'It's good quality. They even have a replacement bag of nuts attached in case anything goes wrong and you lose some'.

GRAHAM: 'It's a nice one. About how many nuts are in that bag by the way?'

ERIC: 'I don't know but there's loads'.

GRAHAM: 'Hey mate, if patients from a mental hospital walked onto a squirrels' nudist beach during an almond finger eating contest, you'd see less 'nuts', ey?!

ERIC: 'H'har har. Would ya ever feck off out of that'!

SCENE FROM A BUS—JAMMY HAS JUST GOT ON AT A STOP
AND SEES HIS MATE BUZZ WHO'S READING A BOOK.

JAMMY: 'Alright, Buzz'.

BUZZ: 'Story, Jammy. Nice day out, isn't it?'

JAMMY: 'Yeah, it's glorious. What's that you're reading?'

BUZZ: 'Oh, it's one written by Joe 'The Bull' Cullen'.

JAMMY: 'He's not really my cup of tea. He's full of it'.

BUZZ: 'I know. It's not that good a read'.

JAMMY: 'He's from Clontarf (on Dublin's north side), isn't
                he?'

BUZZ: 'He is'.

JAMMY: 'Hey, the gaelic for Clontarf is 'Cluain Tarbh'
                which means 'the bull of the meadow', right?'

BUZZ: 'Yeah, that's correct. The 'bull' of 'The Bull' of
                'the bull of the meadow' mate'!

JAMMY: 'H'har har. Very true. You're looking rather tired
                if you don't mind me saying'.

BUZZ: 'I may as well tell ya. I've been messing around
                with my medication for anxiety depression and
                I've been waking up at four in the morning. It's
                my own fault but I'm back on it now. I had taken
                too much of it which had me another type of
                anxious so I decided to stay off it but I went to
                my G.P. and I'm on the right dosage now. I hope
                you believe me when I say I am responsible'.

Cormac G. McDermott, BA, MEconSc

JAMMY: 'Of course. I understand pal. Goodness me, four in the morning. That's the middle of the night. You could have cooked the final meal of a psycho worm which was on death row before it was put out to be executed by the early bird'!

BUZZ: 'Bahahaha. You're a gas man, Jam'!

SCENE FROM A TRAVEL AGENTS—NICOLE AND PHELIM ARE
PLANNING TO BOOK A HOLIDAY.

NICOLE: 'I'd love to go to the U.S. next Summer, Phelim'.

PHELIM: 'Yeah, I think I would too'.

NICOLE: 'It's a vast country. There are so many options'.

PHELIM: 'I don't fancy visiting major cities or anything.
             I'd prefer something a little more relaxing but
             adventurous maybe'.

NICOLE: 'The whole New York, L.A. thing etc doesn't
             appeal to me either'.

PHELIM: 'I'd really like to see the Grand Canyon, Mount
             Rushmore and so on'.

NICOLE: 'We could rent out a log cabin and go fishing or
             something along those lines'.

PHELIM: 'That would be ace, Nicole'.

NICOLE: 'Although, come to think of it, I wouldn't be
             at ease as we might get attacked by a bear or
             something'.

PHELIM: 'Mmm. I see what you mean, but listen, the
             reason they attack humans is because they are
             fed up hearing the phrase 'Does a bear sh*t in
             the woods?' so they frighten people when they
             see us to show that we do it too'!

NICOLE: 'Indeed! Bears probably humour each other by saying 'Do humans sh*t themselves in the woods when they see us?' Right?'!

PHELIM: 'True'!

THE COUPLE GIGGLE AWAY TO THEMSELVES.

SCENE FROM AN OFFICE—FIONA HAS CALLED HER HUSBAND
(DOUG).

FIONA: 'Hi darling'.

DOUG: 'Hiya love. What time will you be home?'

FIONA: 'I'm just finishing up. I should be there by six'.

DOUG: 'No probs. I'm cooking dinner as we speak'.

FIONA: 'Oh, lovely. What are you preparing?'

DOUG: 'Lamb casserole with mash potato'.

FIONA: 'Yum. That's something to look forward to'.

DOUG: 'I've actually been in the kitchen for most of the
            afternoon'.

FIONA: 'Really? What else were you making?'

DOUG: 'Ginger snaps'.

FIONA: 'Ginger snaps? What are they?'

DOUG: 'They're a type of biscuit'.

FIONA: 'Ginger snaps, ey? Are you sure you're talking
            about a type of biscuit and not a pair of red-
            headed twins who might appear on a deck of
            cards?'!

DOUG: 'Bahahaha. You're a character, Fi. I'll see you in
            a couple of hours, love'.

FIONA: 'B'bye honey'.

SCENE FROM A LIVING ROOM—NICOLE AND PHELIM ARE WATCHING A TELEVISION PROGRAMME FROM THE U.S. WHERE A ROW IS BREWING BETWEEN MALE POLITICIANS AND FEMINISTS.

NICOLE: 'This discussion is beginning to get very heated, Phelim'.

PHELIM: 'It is. I have to say I'm on the feminists side'.

NICOLE: 'Why is that?'

PHELIM: 'Politics has been a male-dominated arena for a long time now. We need to encourage more females to get involved and redress the balance'.

NICOLE: 'Yeah, I think women should enter this sphere as the world is in a state because things haven't been stable enough alright'.

PHELIM: 'I've told you before how I feel about the world. I don't like secular politics, a non-fundamentally regulated financial world (and the explosion of finance in general), a lot of games, betting offices, empty religious doctrine and so on. God love the poor women. The world has been established and they are probably frightened all the nonsense that exists which rendered them unequal will be used as weapons to hurt them if they try to elevate themselves. My heart really goes out to them'.

NICOLE: 'I see where you are coming from'.

PHELIM: 'It strikes me feminism only exists as a reaction to worldliness created by males who don't want to mend their ways. I detest what this sort of stuff does to men who don't have the genius to question it and the female mind-frame. I'd

22

say they only want to liberate both genders and educate us into living a freer lifestyle'.

NICOLE: 'Those women in tweed suits would love you'!

PHELIM: 'I'd imagine they desire that they rediscover males to be a mystery in terms of their spirituality rather than confuse them and get at the non-love aspects of their sexual nature by proponentising worldliness, ey?'

NICOLE: 'Wow. That's probably very true. I'd say they'd admire you for coming out with something like that'!

PHELIM: 'Do feminists get involved in relationships with men? I understand why they dislike what a lot of men proponentise and they are probably fed up at this stage. Some of them have lovely minds and it would be sad if they had nobody of their own to love and nobody special to love them back as therapy'.

NICOLE: 'Heads of cabbage tend to have 'no body' of their own to love either but at least they usually go well with ribs although come to think of it they could be from a male chauvinist 'pig', right?'!

PHELIM CHUCKLES.

PHELIM: 'Ah. I reckon you females are probably more right at times than what you are given credit for in certain respects'!

NICOLE: 'Aw, thanks hun but some of us are vindictive bitches too'!

THE COUPLE KISS EACH OTHER.

SCENE FROM A KITCHEN—NICOLE IS CHATTING AWAY TO
HER SON (TOMMY).

NICOLE: 'How was school today, Tommy?'

TOMMY: 'It was very interesting, mam. We were learning
               all about the start of the European Union'.

NICOLE: 'Oh, very good. Did you play gaelic football after
               school?'

TOMMY: 'I did. We beat St. Finbarr's, Ballymun (on
               Dublin's north side) in the quarter-final of the
               Championship'.

NICOLE: 'Did you get on the score-sheet?'

TOMMY: 'I kicked a goal and four points. I played very
               well and got our Man of the Match'.

NICOLE: 'Wuhoo. That's my boy! I suppose you have a kit
               to be washed, ey?'

TOMMY: 'Yeah, it's in the utilities room'.

NICOLE: 'I may as well wash it now'.

NICOLE LEAVES THE KITCHEN AS PHELIM ENTERS THROUGH THE
        HALL DOOR FROM WORK.

NICOLE: 'For feck sake, Tommy. This place looks like you
               were in a mud bath. Come in here and mop it all
               up this minute'.

TOMMY: 'Okay, mam. Where is the black bucket?'

NICOLE: 'I don't know. Go look for it out the back'.

PHELIM: 'I'd say it's within kicking distance of your deceased grand-mother's grave anyway, son'!

PHELIM AND TOMMY LAUGH.

NICOLE: 'I heard that, Phelim'!

SCENE FROM A WORK PLACE—NICOLE AND BUZZ ARE
CHATTING.

NICOLE: 'How's your pal, Jammy, keeping these days,
               Buzz?'

BUZZ: 'Ah, he's not too bad. Still trying to find work but
               he's keeping the sunny side out'.

NICOLE: 'You're the lucky one having got a job here, ey?'

BUZZ: 'I am I suppose but I'd imagine he'll be offered
               something before long as he's very employable'.

NICOLE: 'Tell him I was asking for him and hope he picks
               up a job soon, won't you?'

BUZZ: 'I will of course'.

NICOLE GETS DISTRACTED.

NICOLE: 'Who's that girl over there? I don't think I've seen
               her before'.

BUZZ: 'Oh, that's that new girl we've just brought down
               from production. She's from Liverpool'.

NICOLE: 'She looks very friendly. What's her name and I'll
               go over, introduce myself and welcome her?'

BUZZ: 'Becky Leckie'!

NICOLE: 'What?'!

BUZZ: 'I'm not joking! Scousers are fecking comical,
               ey?'!

NICOLE: 'They are! Although the company probably only took her on hoping that they could plug her into the wall in an attempt to bring down the heating and lighting bills, right?'!

THE PAIR CRACK UP.

SCENE FROM A LIVING ROOM—JAMMY HAS CALLED AROUND
TO SEE MAXI. THEY ARE WATCHING A NEWS CHANNEL.

VOICE FROM
THE
TELEVISION: 'A suicide bomber has blown himself up at an
army checkpoint in Kabul today. There have
reportedly been seven casualties and dozens
injured in the explosion'.

JAMMY: 'This sort of stuff is always going on in the Middle
Easy, Maxi'.

MAXI: 'I know. Going off in a tangent a bit, Muslims
are probably right regarding certain aspects of
Western culture but that surely can't be the
proper way to hunger and thirst for justice'.

JAMMY: 'They have to let us live the way we want to
aswell. I'm a devout follower of Jesus and I don't
like the way some Muslims are trying to enforce
their religion on primarily Christian countries.
We're entitled to our views too'.

MAXI: 'Yeah. I agree. However, I don't know what
to make of Roman Catholicism linking up with
Islam, do you?'

JAMMY: 'No, I don't. Wexford and all that is referred
to as the 'Sunny South East' but before long it
might become the 'SUNNI South East' if you get
what I mean'!

MAXI: 'I cop what you're on about alright and if you
think about it, Donegal and that part of the
country might become the 'Ban-SHIA North West'
if this does happen, right?'!

SCENE FROM A BAR—PHELIM AND JOHN ARE HAVING A DRINK.

PHELIM: 'What's that non-alcoholic beer like, John?'

JOHN: 'It's lovely, Phelim. There's a little bit of lemon in it. Would you like to try some?'

PHELIM: 'No, you're alright thanks'.

JOHN: 'It's really light. I doubt it will give you a hangover like that soapy Hordenger'.

PHELIM: 'I heard that stuff's lethal'.

JOHN: 'It is. Four bottles of that drink would do even more damage than a whole day's session'.

PHELIM: 'Who's that barman who served you by the way?'

JOHN: 'That's Miguel Busquets. He's just moved here from Barcelona'.

PHELIM: 'Busquets, ey? His name sounds like what you'd call a group of females who play musical instruments and look for loose change off people in the streets of Spanish city centres, ey?'!

JOHN: 'Ha ha. What sort of wisecracks are you going to come out with after a few more pints ya made thing'!

SCENE FROM A LIVING ROOM—ERIC HAS CALLED AROUND TO SEE GRAHAM AND WATCH A GAME OF SOCCER.

THE BELL RINGS AND GRAHAM ANSWERS THE DOOR.

GRAHAM: 'Come on in, Eric. The game is only twelve minutes old'.

ERIC: 'Cheers mate. Have I missed anything?'

GRAHAM: 'Rovers had a half decent chance to take the lead about five minutes ago but it's been a bit of a slow start'.

VOICE FROM
THE TELLY: 'The big man has started but Jack King could spoil his clean sheet with a handling performance like that'.

ERIC
(Laughing): 'Am I hearing things?'!

GRAHAM: 'What?'

ERIC: 'Were you not listening to the commentator?'!

GRAHAM: 'I was, yeah, but I don't know what has you so amused'.

ERIC: 'He said 'the big man has started but j*cking could spoil his clean sheet with a handling performance like that''!

ERIC KEEPS GIGGLING. THE JOKE REGISTERS WITH GRAHAM.

GRAHAM
(Chuckling):   'Oh, I get it! Somebody should tell that bloke we
                only want to know about on the field matters
                and not if he has a 'pedal' every time he
                changes his bed linen, right?'!

ERIC: 'That's it! I wonder if anyone else has picked up
                on what he said?'!

GRAHAM: 'He's never going to live that one down'!

BOTH MEN CONTINUE TO CRACK UP.

SCENE FROM A STREET—JAMMY HAS BUMPED INTO HIS
NEIGHBOUR (PHELIM).

JAMMY: 'Story, Phelim. How's Nicole and your kid'.

PHELIM: 'They're grand thanks. Where are you coming from? You look like you've had a few'.

JAMMY: 'You're right. I've had a few scoops'.

PHELIM: 'Where are you getting the money to be drinking on a school night when you're not working?'

JAMMY: 'Buzz got a new job and gave me fifty euro'.

PHELIM: 'Fair play to him. That's a sound thing to do'.

JAMMY: 'It is. We're great mates'.

PHELIM: 'Yeah, I know that. Where did you have your bevs?'

JAMMY: 'The Station House in Raheny village'.

PHELIM: 'That's a nice spot. The staff are sound. They call that place the Stat Ho for short'.

JAMMY: 'Why? Do they expect to bump into a lady of the night in the place who'll tell them there's a high 'probability' she'll give them a ride for free if they buy her a few glasses of wine or something?'!

PHELIM: 'Feck off ya lunatic although the place is closing down, opening up again under new management and is going to be re-named as The Cock & Bull'!

JAMMY: 'Oh, really. So the Stat Ho is going to turn into a Cock & Bull. She must be getting a sex change! Who knows it might even be called The Raheny Lady Boy some time in the future'!

PHELIM: 'Bahahaha. You never know, it could do'!

SCENE FROM A KITCHEN—SPARKS AND PLUG ARE IN JAMMY'S HOUSE.

SPARKS: 'How long is Jammy gone now?'

PLUG: 'I'd say about fifty five minutes. You're really hungry, aren't you? I can tell by ya'.

SPARKS: 'You're right. I worked up an appetite in the gym before coming over'.

PLUG: 'I wonder what he's going to get'.

THE MEN ARE ALERTED BY THE SOUND OF KEYS RATTLING IN THE PORCH.

SPARKS: 'That should be him'.

JAMMY ENTERS THE KITCHEN HOLDING A PAPER BUCKET AND SOME BAGS.

PLUG: 'What took ya mate?'

JAMMY: 'I got talking to the Polish bloke who lives next door. I didn't want to be rude. He kept me yapping'.

SPARKS: 'Is he a nice guy?'

JAMMY: 'Ah, yeah. Legia is sound. He cleared the snow that was lying outside my gate last Winter'.

PLUG: 'His name is Legia? Well, I'm glad he didn't take a 'leg eeh ya' chicken out of that bucket you've just put on the table as Sparks looks like he might faint with the hunger'!

SPARKS CHUCKLES.

JAMMY: 'Don't give up the day job, Plug'.

SCENE FROM A BAR IN NEW ORLEANS—DOUG AND FIONA
ARE ON VACATION.

DOUG: 'There's some cool-sounding music coming from over there, Fi. Let's go and check it out'.

FIONA: 'Sure. Why not?'

THEY ENTER A BAR AND SIT DOWN.

DOUG: 'What are you having? The usual?'

FIONA: 'No. I think I'll go for a glass of red this time'.

DOUG: 'A glass of red it is'.

DOUG GOES UP TO THE BAR AND RETURNS WITH THEIR DRINKS.

FIONA: 'Thanks, Doug. Well, cheers'.

THE COUPLE CLINK GLASSES.

DOUG: 'The music is only coming from the juke box. I thought there may have been a live act on'.

FIONA: 'To be honest, I'm glad. I wasn't in the humour for anything too intense'.

DOUG: 'There seems to be a lot of history in this joint. I mean, look at all the memorabilia on the walls'.

FIONA: 'I'd say there's been a lot of famous heads in here alright'.

DOUG SPOTS SOMETHING.

DOUG

(Pointing):   'Hey, check out the platinum disc signed by Rusty Carmichael'.

FIONA: 'I've never heard of him. Who is he?'

DOUG: 'He's an award winning guitarist'.

FIONA: 'He's obviously a smoothie when it comes to the blues, ey?'

DOUG: 'Smoothie when it comes to the blues? That's just like saying he's a fruity yogurt drink when it comes to conservative Chelsea fans who are schmangeable'!

FIONA: 'Baha. Feck off out of that'!

THE COUPLE CONTINUE TO CHAT.

SCENE FROM A BEDROOM—NICOLE AND PHELIM ARE CHATTING.

NICOLE: 'Did you tell Tommy to turn off his laptop and go to sleep'.

PHELIM: 'I did. He's a good little fella, ey?'

NICOLE: 'Yeah, he really is a blessing to us. Do you think it's time we tried for another, love?'

PHELIM: 'It would be nice if he was to have a little brother or sister'.

NICOLE: 'We are financially quite stable so why not?'

PHELIM: 'You never know. If I was to ever get a promotion in work, we could start a whole tribe of us'!

NICOLE: 'Ah, now hold on. One step at a time. After we have the next child, I reckon we might want to call it a day'.

PHELIM: 'Well, I have to say I think 'A Day' is a fecking stupid name to be giving to a baby myself but if you insist'!

NICOLE: 'Give over'!

SCENE FROM A STREET—GRAHAM HAS BUMPED INTO ERIC WHO IS CHUCKLING AWAY TO HIMSELF.

GRAHAM: 'Alright, Eric'.

ERIC GATHERS HIMSELF.

ERIC: 'Story, Graham. What's the craic with ya?'

ERIC CONTINUES GIGGLING.

GRAHAM: 'I'm on the way up to visit my folks. What on earth has you so giddy?'

ERIC: 'Aw, stop. I've just been in Connolly Station (in Dublin's city centre) and overheard a conversation between a few rail workers'.

GRAHAM: 'Well, go on. Tell me'.

ERIC: 'This bloke introduces a Spanish guy to one fella. The dude says 'Hey, this is Pablo Michu our new driver on the Dublin to Sligo line. Pablo, this is Bill Carr'. Now that's not the funny part but what is is that the witty Dub cracked 'Heeaw, Pablo. I heard your brother 'Pleased To' is forever shaking the hands of people he's never met before too'! But fair play to the Spaniard he retorts 'Me Michu choo and you, Carr, does be very vroom vroom'! The three of them cracked up! It was fecking comical'!

GRAHAM SEES THE FUNNY SIDE TOO.

GRAHAM: 'Stuff like that would put you in a good humour alright! I'm not surprised you've been laughing away to yourself mate'!

SCENE FROM A BUTCHER'S SHOP IN DUBLIN—DOUG ENTERS THE PREMISES AND A WOMAN IS AT THE COUNTER.

WOMAN: 'Give us a joint of beef der love'.

ASSISTANT: 'Sure. No probs'.

THE ASSISTANT REACHES DOWN INTO THE CABINET AND GETS THE BEEF. HE SHOWS IT TO THE LADY.

ASSISTANT: 'How does that look to you?'

WOMAN: 'Yeah, dat looks luvlee. Oi'ill take et'. (Yeah, that looks lovely. I'll take it).

ASSISTANT: 'That will be ten euro please'.

WOMAN: 'Wud jeh evvaw f*ck off! Were dih yeh tink oi'id geh ten euro for a piece of meeh from?'! (Would you ever f*ck off. Where do you think I'd get ten euro for a piece of meat from?!).

THE ASSISTANT IS TAKEN ABACK.

ASSISTANT: 'Okay then, eight euro'.

THE LADY PROCEEDS TO TAKE A TEN EURO NOTE OUT OF HER PURSE AND HAS THE CHEEK TO WAIT AROUND FOR THE TWO EURO CHANGE!

DOUG STRUGGLES TO CONTAIN HIS LAUGHTER BUT CAN'T WAIT TO TELL FIONA WHAT HE HAS WITNESSED!

SCENE FROM A CONVENIENT STORE—NICOLE AND PHELIM ARE SHOPPING FOR GROCERIES.

NICOLE: 'What veg would you like to have with the corned beef, Phelim?'

PHELIM: 'I'd love some cabbage but I already had that with the roast chicken dinner you did for me at the weekend so I suppose I'll go for carrots and sprouts'.

NICOLE: 'No probs. C'mon, the vegetable counter is over here'.

PHELIM: 'They look like a nice bag of sprouts there'.

NICOLE: 'Well, grab that net then'.

PHELIM PICKS THEM UP.

NICOLE: 'Check out the label and see where they are from'.

PHELIM: 'Oh, it says here 'Produce of Belgium''.

NICOLE: 'We really should be buying Irish goods. Who's the grower?'

PHELIM: 'The company is called Herdild'.

NICOLE: 'Sweet Jesus, sounds like a Dublin newspaper seller'!

PHELIM IS A LITTLE STUMPED.

NICOLE: 'Just think of those people selling the papers back in the day'!

PHELIM: 'I'm still a little puzzled, Nicole'.

NICOLE (In a
strong accent): 'Herdild aw Press'! (Herald or Press!).

PHELIM COPS WHAT NICOLE IS ON ABOUT AND CHUCKLES.

SCENE FROM A HOUSE—SPARKS HAS CALLED TO SEE HIS BROTHER (PLUG).

SPARKS: 'Alright, Plug'.

PLUG: 'Ah, Sparks. C'mon in. Would you like a cuppa?'

SPARKS: 'Nah, you're grand thanks. Just had one before I left the house'.

PLUG: 'So, what's the craic with ya?'

SPARKS: 'Nothing much going on with me. And yourself?'

PLUG: 'Things are fairly quiet with me too'.

SPARKS: 'Hey. You're next door neighbour is a bit of alright? Who is she?'

PLUG: 'That's Maria Kuyt. She's Dutch. She's very attractive, ey?'

SPARKS: 'You can say that again. Maria Kuyt and her twin sister 'It's a Knock', right?'!

PLUG: 'She's a knock Kuyt for sure'!

SPARKS: 'I tell ya when I go home, I'll be tempted to knock one Kuyt because of her. Too right I will'!

PLUG: 'Give it a rest ya dirty fecker'!

THE TWO MEN CHUCKLE.

SCENE FROM A GARDEN—JOHN AND MAXI ARE WEEDING
THE DRIVEWAY.

JOHN: 'This is doing my back in, Maxi'.

MAXI: 'You'll feel better having done some work. Your dinner will taste even nicer mate'.

JOHN: 'We've been at this for an hour now. When was the last time this cobble-locking was cleaned'.

MAXI: 'About ten months ago. I don't like doing it. It's a job that I find stressful. You're very good for helping me out with it'.

JOHN: 'No probs. Do you know what gets me stressed?'

MAXI: 'What?'

JOHN: 'Those news channels that apply spin'.

MAXI: 'Don't get me fecking started. I end up confused if I tune in'.

JOHN: 'It confuses me too. Television is a very powerful medium and peoples' welfare should be taken into consideration by them more, ey?

MAXI: 'You're bang on there. If I wanted to be entertained by spin, I'd put my favourite cd on'!

JOHN: 'Ha ha. More spinning done by the feckers than a break-dancing fly on a carousel which has just been sprayed with insecticide, ey?'!

MAXI: 'Yeah! H'har har'!

SCENE FROM A HOUSE—DOUG AND FIONA ARE CHATTING AWAY.

DOUG: 'Would you like a foot massage, Fi?'

FIONA: 'Oh, that would be lovely, Doug. I've hardly sat down all day'.

DOUG BEGINS TO MASSAGE FIONA.

DOUG: 'How does that feel?'

FIONA: 'It's very soothing darling'.

DOUG: 'Have you thought about what you'd like us to do at the weekend'.

FIONA: 'To be honest, I haven't. I've been up to my eyes in work'.

DOUG: 'I was thinking we could go to see Hall & Oates. They're playing The Olympia Saturday evening'.

FIONA: 'Oh, were we not expecting Donal and Elaine for dinner this Saturday?'

DOUG: 'Ah, yeah. You're right. It had slipped my mind but we could suggest going to the gig instead, ey?'

FIONA: 'I'll call, Elaine'.

FIONA PICKS UP HER MOBILE AND PRETENDS TO CALL ELAINE. THE FICTITIOUS CONVERSATION ENDS. SHE SEEMS A LITTLE DISAPPOINTED.

DOUG: 'What did she say?'

FIONA: 'I Can't Go To That Nor Can Doh'!

DOUG: 'That's a pity'.

FIONA BEGINS TO GIGGLE. IT DAWNS OF DOUG WHAT SHE WAS REFERRING TO.

DOUG: 'Ha ha ha. You got me there'!

FIONA: 'Hold on, I'll call her for real this time and ask can she and Donal leave it for another time. I'd really like to go to the event'.

DOUG: 'Yeah, go on. Do that pet. I'd love to see them live too although you could suggest they come with us as I said, ey?'

FIONA: 'Good idea sweetie'.

SCENE FROM A CAFE—ERIC AND GRAHAM ARE HAVING A CAPPUCCINO.

ERIC: 'This is a great little place, ey?'

GRAHAM: 'Yeah. There's always people in it'.

ERIC: 'I'd say it's a goldmine, the International Financial Services Centre is just around the corner'.

GRAHAM: 'Oh, I'd say it is alright. That almond slice you have there looks tasty. My Danish was very fresh'.

ERIC: 'Good. I love anything with nuts'.

GRAHAM: 'Speaking of nuts would you like to hear a joke mate?'

ERIC: 'Sure. Go on'.

GRAHAM: 'What would you call two nuts against Hazel?'

ERIC: 'I don't know'.

GRAHAM: 'Hazelnuts. What would you call two nuts against a chimpanzee?'

ERIC: 'I suppose it would be monkey nuts, ey?'

GRAHAM: 'That's right. What would you call two nuts against GOD?'

ERIC: 'Feck this, I don't know. Well, what about GOD nuts?

GRAHAM: 'No. The antichrist and the false prophet'!

ERIC: 'G'wan owadah ya bleedin' mad thing'!

SCENE FROM A PUB—JOHN AND MAXI ARE TALKING ABOUT WORK.

JOHN: 'Things are getting nasty down the docks, Maxi'.

MAXI: 'Why? What's up?'

JOHN: 'Because of all the cut-backs there's fewer hours to be worked and the men are beginning to grapple over the hours on our schedule'.

MAXI: 'Does it affect you directly?'

JOHN: 'It does. I'm not in there long so I'm not the first in line for the labour'.

MAXI: 'Is there anything you can do about it?'

JOHN: 'I could actually ask for fewer hours and get assistance from the Government but I don't want to be doing that'.

MAXI: 'Fair play to you for being so honest. You obviously don't want to be a further burden on the tax-payer'.

JOHN: 'Cheers. I'm not too bad though. Some of the lads down there have large families and have lots of kids to take care of. There was murder last Friday when Psycho Tierney found out his work-load was being lightened'.

MAXI: 'You told me about him before. He's a bit of a hard nut, right?'

JOHN: 'Hard is the word for him alright. I'm telling ya, he's so bleedin' hard, he'd make bastard mahogany cooking rottweiler stew for maraging steel in the Parkway Tavern in Sheffield during Halloween look soft'!

BOTH MEN BEGIN TO CHUCKLE.

SCENE FROM A HOUSE—ANGEL AND COUNSELLOR ARE HAVING A CHAT.

ANGEL: 'Did you enjoy your breakfast darling?'

COUNSELLOR: 'It was delicious. You know I'm only falling deeper in love with you, don't you?'

ANGEL: 'I'm very assured about the fact that you're a peace-maker and wouldn't empower yourself in an illicit way'.

COUNSELLOR: 'I'm so glad you feel confident in that respect. You're so kind the way you ease any potential guilt I might feel'.

ANGEL: 'I know you appreciate everything I do for you but you do something similar don't forget'.

COUNSELLOR: 'Thank you so much. Jesus Christ advised that we should refrain from criticising one another because we'd have the same fault to at least the same degree (if not more). But if you open your mind, maybe people shouldn't be so quick to over compliment others as one would probably possess the same quality to at least a similar extent, ey?'!

ANGEL: 'I agree. Love your neighbour as yourself and all that. Now, before you call me a pet and dote, you ought to know that's what you are too'!

THE COUPLE GIVE EACH OTHER A KISS.

ANGEL: 'What are we going to do tonight?'

COUNSELLOR: 'I haven't really thought about what I'd like us to do'.

ANGEL: 'How about a trip to the flicks?'

COUNSELLOR: 'Yeah, why not? We haven't been there in a while. What would you like to see?'

ANGEL: 'We could go to see 'Alike Yet Unlike''.

COUNSELLOR: 'Fair enough. Ah, hold on a second, I heard that film contains a lot of nudity. If I'm stressed out, it could be far too racey'!

ANGEL: 'I'll keep your spirits up'!

COUNSELLOR: 'I'm not sure. Camp can be humorous but neither males nor females should be taking their 'Rovers 'n' Bohs' off in public'!

ANGEL: 'It's all just a bit of harmless fun. There's some women who'll be starkers too! Don't worry, we'll have a great laugh'!

SCENE FROM A STREET—TONY HAS CALLED TO THE DOOR OF HIS NEIGHBOUR (DAR DAR).

TONY: 'Alright, Dar Dar'.

DAR DAR: 'Howaya, Tony. What did that fella who lives on his own in the corner house who says he's the Counsellor tell you this time?'!

TONY: 'You're not going to believe some of the things he was saying. I wrote what I could down'!

DAR DAR: 'Go on, I'm bracing myself'!

TONY: 'He started off with Jesus' Sermon on the Mount again. He isn't one hundred per cent certain but he senses he actually might be the Light of the World because he is the Spirit which is signified by a Lamp and that would be the source of all light. His light definitely shines through the Church anyway'!

DAR DAR: 'It's making perfect sense'!

TONY: 'He also believes he could be the Salt of the Earth with his Spirit being the salt. He says he lives inside every living entity and if the individual was to forgo their own spirituality, his Spirit would be diluted within them and they would thus become apostates which would only be good enough to be 'thrown out and trampled underfoot by men'!

DAR DAR: 'That's powerful'!

TONY: 'He continued that the Lord's allusion to Salt and Light came immediately after the last Beatitude when Jesus acknowledged (because he as the future Counsellor would have been in His prophesising sub-conscious) that he is Blessed along with Yahweh and Yeshua and foresaw what would go in his life during a time of apostasy. That would have influenced what came after his revelation of him being the source of Salt and Light'!

DAR DAR: 'I'm fecking speechless'!

TONY: 'He thinks Christ may have incorporated him into His teachings throughout His public ministry because he's a genius and, to re-iterate, was in His prophesising sub-conscious'!

DAR DAR: 'This is blowing my mind away, Tony'!

TONY: 'I know, it's seriously intriguing stuff, ey?'!

DAR DAR: 'Too right it is'!

TONY: 'He is His Father's Spirit for sure mate'!

DAR DAR: 'I'm not selling this house and neither should you sell yours. When he goes off to Heaven in a blaze of glory, they'll be worth a small fortune'!

TONY: 'The bloke is a national treasure'!

DAR DAR: 'That's a very true statement. What else had he got to say? I can't get enough of this. It's amazing'!

TONY: 'He says he's in a very unhappy place and just wants the pet, dote and exuder of angelic-ness he developed a massive crush on sixteen years ago to be his best friend'!

DAR DAR: 'Ah. All this bloke needs is love'!

TONY: 'He expressed that she is an adorable and delightful girlish, baby-mawmmy and has been dominating his thoughts for a long time now'!

DAR DAR: 'He's in love with her'!

TONY: ''She's the most wonderful specimen of femininity' he added'!

DAR DAR: 'Sounds like she's nice'!

TONY: 'She's easily the most beautiful girl who has ever showed an interest in him and the nearest thing he's seen to an angel here on planet earth, he sighed'!

DAR DAR: 'Tasty babe, ey?'!

TONY: 'He said she'd put a horn on impotent fog even while it was taking a cold shower'!

DAR DAR: 'They'd probably make a really cute couple'!

TONY: 'He told me he has always had to learn from life the hard way and hopes she can help him deal with his anxieties and the fact that he is going to love his life not so much so as to shrink from death'!

DAR DAR: 'He's definitely a romantic'!

TONY: 'He's feeling he is going to fall head over heels, hopelessly and helplessly in love with her. He's prophesising that she could be taken away in the rapture of the church which will break his heart because she'll be his main reason for living'!

DAR DAR: 'I see'!

TONY: 'He says he'll be comforted knowing that she is in Heaven but he'll be missing her so much, that martyrdom cannot come around quickly enough for him'!

DAR DAR: 'This guy is brave'!

TONY: 'Although he's also sensing it's more likely she could be still here on earth but saying goodbye to her will be a wrench because she would have been his greatest ever ally on this planet. 'Because the world cannot accept me, I've hardly even known what love is throughout my life', he continued'!

DAR DAR: 'Ah'!

TONY: 'He said he didn't want to be forcing things too much but he's in knowledge of something in relation to 'The Spouse' and it could be her that the prophets (or maybe Yahweh Himself) was referring to. 'It might be in reference to 'The Little Book' and she could very possibly help me promote my work or could do it herself after my resurrection', he added'!

DAR DAR: ''The Little Book' that will have our stomachs churning as was prophesised which you told me about the last time, ey?'!

TONY: 'Yeah'!

DAR DAR: 'I wonder what it will be about this book that will make our stomachs churn. It could be fairly funny, ey?'!

TONY: 'I can't think of it being anything else mate'!

DAR DAR: 'I must look up his work on the internet. It has me very intrigued'!

TONY: 'Me too. However, he was telling me all his wounds and all that he has in common with 'the son of perdition' because of his own transgressions will be used to induce him into hating his life. He admits he has sinned out of his own volition at times but he doesn't feel too guilty about it as he suffers from schizophrenia and has never been anything other than a prisoner in his circumstances because of the media and to a distressing future since his infancy'!

DAR DAR: 'I must admit I'm fascinated by the man, Tony'!

TONY: 'He thinks it was maybe his own fault in certain respects to have been from a working class background and entered middle class spheres as he thinks he may have gone against Scripture advice by doing this. It was a case of power over vulnerability. However, there may have been no issues at all but for the fact that the other media men were repressing him and perversifying his character and circumstances. Deep down he has always admired how refined he regards a lot of them to be. In addition, he felt for the females and it has broken his heart that they seemed to get a power-buzz and a bit of a thrill out of making a scapegoat out of him when he was on their side more often than they had realised just because he was vulnerable due to his confusion and innocence levels. In general, it was the other media men who had him and people the way they were and it's nobody's fault but he regards much of it as being very secular'!

DAR DAR: 'It's a little unfortunate for him alright'!

TONY: 'He continued that he doesn't understand certain things but he accepts it all happened at a dangerous age for him (which it does for all young people) and what he can't help get the impression was a fairly secular-increasing time'!

DAR DAR: 'Things are different now alright'!

TONY: 'When it came to the females he thinks he understands what their plight to elevate themselves within society and what their view of justice was but, to re-iterate, they weren't really interested in trying to understand him in his opinion. Although he can't help feeling that he is a little bit different'!

DAR DAR: 'He probably just feels completely violated'!

TONY: 'He said where their mind-frames were upset him and he was determined to bring them to a position where they would be appreciated for the attitudes of their hearts and minds. This in turn would make them more emotionally and physically attractive but they made a scapegoat out of him concurrently'!

DAR DAR: 'He seems to understand women better than the average bloke'!

TONY: 'He advised me that he wants to learn what females are sensitive to so that he can become sensitive to it also in order to become a better person'!

DAR DAR: 'That's very nice on his behalf'!

TONY: 'He went on he's been dragged down by power-playing mediocrity'!

DAR DAR: 'Well, as I said to you before, if he is the Counsellor, he fully evidences the high standards Yahweh has'!

TONY: 'He revealed to me any time he has tried to communicate regarding the injustices that he feels were levelled against him, he's been abused, told he is still going on about things or that it is all water under the bridge'!

DAR DAR: 'He's never been able to give his side of the story, has he?'!

TONY: 'He insists that people found it easy to communicate about him but were not as eager to communicate with him'!

DAR DAR: 'That would be very frustrating'!

TONY: ''Practically all I've ever got is the contempt and the insinuation', he added. 'It was all very confusing' he continued'!

DAR DAR: 'They must have had their own issues which disenabled them from connecting better with him'!

TONY: 'You've taken his words right out of my mouth'!

DAR DAR: 'He's right'!

TONY: 'His opinion is that love is a battle-field but with real people nobody is superficially wounded.

57

People allow each other to give their side of the story and if they fail to agree, that's just the way it is'!

DAR DAR: 'That's the proper way to conduct proceedings alright'!

TONY: 'Do you remember I told you that a guest minister on a programme called 'Extreme Prophetic' on The GOD Channel almost broke down in tears when it was being revealed to the man the way he was being treated by those he was coming into contact with?'!

DAR DAR: 'Yeah, I do remember what you told me'!

TONY: 'He was telling me it was aired about seven years ago. What the gentleman said was 'You're a young man. You've been caught up in a homosexual sin pattern. You were dealing with people who were making themselves out to be victims'. It was at this stage he became emotional when the cruelness of everything was being revealed to him. He continued 'you were preyed upon. And I'm not saying P-R-A-Y-E-D but P-R-E-Y-E-D. On behalf of these people I apologise. You KNOW the Lord''!

DAR DAR: 'Well, if this was being revealed to this man on the television from God, it's obviously true what this bloke was saying to you about how he was being treated'!

TONY: 'He just feels he's constantly been given things to think about'!

DAR DAR: 'Maybe what Jesus said about the world not being able to accept him is true'!

TONY: 'He says God sometimes takes the weak things of the world to shame the strong and the foolish things to shame the wise. He says when the Scriptures state 'we keep obedient every thought and every pretention that sets itself up against the knowledge of the Lord etc', it's all meant to start with the individual establishing the truth and discipline within themselves. However, it is good to furnish those who may lack a little knowledge and build them up in accordance to their needs'!

DAR DAR: 'I know what you mean'!

TONY: 'However, you must respect peoples' intuition too, he added'!

DAR DAR: 'As he has said before, 'no one individual is the sole blessee of wisdom' and all that'!

TONY: 'He didn't know what to make of peoples' unnatural-ness'!

DAR DAR: 'Yeah, being on the end of that sort of stuff can be confusing'!

TONY: ''It's a bit like subjugation of innocence' as he put it but he respects that they would possess some knowledge he doesn't even though he's the Counsellor'!

DAR DAR: 'It's a serious issue'!

TONY: 'He says the Golden Rule is that you have to treat people how you would wish to be treated yourself'!

DAR DAR: 'With his illness and all that, it sounds like it's all been very cruel on him'!

TONY: 'Although, he went on that he knows these people have regard for him when they had the freedom to choose but he encountered difficulties when he wanted to be free to choose. However, he senses society seems to be different now that the other media men have been removed from their positions as he feels they were trying to turn people against one another'!

DAR DAR: 'I see'!

TONY: 'He continued that he is heart-broken as his adult life has been so trouble-filled and has been more or less totally destroyed. He was telling me he doesn't have much to live for anymore and his illness is very cruel but he is going to keep praying over it in Jesus' Name and that will enable him to overcome it before long'!

DAR DAR: 'This is so sad'!

TONY: 'He's been left feeling very hurt, wounded and violated and just hopes people who know who he is help him to gather up the pieces of a problem-filled life'!

DAR DAR: 'He doesn't feel his life has been his own, does he?'!

TONY: 'He doesn't. And, as I just said to you, some of his future is going to be very disturbing (because of the large history of secular-ness) and it's a difficult thing for him to deal with'!

DAR DAR: 'I feel so sorry for the bloke'!

TONY: 'He knows it wasn't his fault he was making mistakes as the secular media has never done anything but relentlessly trespass upon his life, invade his privacy and violate his very being. He continued that he has hardly ever even known as much as freedom because of it'!

DAR DAR: 'He really has suffered throughout his time on earth mate'!

TONY: ''I've spent my whole life just wanting to be free and keep things open for myself' he explained'!

DAR DAR: 'It's only natural he'd feel that way. There's nobody who wouldn't'!

TONY: 'He's maintaining he's fairly certain the other media men were fuelling peoples' negative opinions of and attitudes towards him despite the fact they were the reason his behaviour was erratic and becoming increasingly so'!

DAR DAR: 'This is all rather upsetting. And the man has always suffered from schizophrenia, has a disorder, eccentric traits plus the mental age of a one year old too. The poor fella'!

TONY: 'Although he's maintaining if he had power over people, knew a lot of their business, adopted an attitude that they needed help from him and gave them things to think about (including by strangers when they moved from one sphere of their lives into the next), maybe they'd make mistakes too. It was as if he wasn't even aware of his own circumstances on many occasions'!

DAR DAR: 'He likes to be in control of what people know about him. He's no different to anybody else.

It's not good that a sufferer of schizophrenia be treated this way'!

TONY: 'I know. He concluded by saying that every sphere he entered into during his twenties he picked up problems. People were making themselves out to be victims. He doesn't feel there was anything normal about what was going on with him'!

DAR DAR: 'It's awful for him. One difficult situation after the next, ey?'!

TONY: 'What Jesus prophesised about the world not being able to accept him is definitely true mate. He's always known this and that's why he was making mistakes'!

DAR DAR: 'I'm very intrigued by the whole media involvement thing. He must have had more to say about his experiences, ey?'!

TONY: 'Yeah. He revealed to me his first memory is of when he was a foetus. In his mind he knew himself he is the Spirit as he can remember convincing himself of it while in his mother's womb. He continued that he didn't know how it was possible but he remembers thinking it in English. He feels it may have been because he has psychic abilities, was prophesising it would be his first language and was speaking in tongues due to his spirituality as the world had not negatively affected him at this point'!

DAR DAR: 'Imagine being able to realise and have the abilities to do that'!

TONY: 'He went on that, because he is a prophet, he thought in his mind 'some people are going to move to make your life a difficulty'. As soon as he thought this, he heard these frightening screams coming from outside his mam. He said he obviously didn't know it was television but he knew that there would be something in the world that these people who were going to conspire against him would use to get to him. He continued that there has been relentless media involvement in his life his entire existence on planet earth'!

DAR DAR: 'Unbelievable precocious-ness and foresight from a foetus. But these people have been removed from their positions now, right?'!

TONY: 'Looking back, he said the media have been kind enough to consider him but with what the other men were doing to him concurrently was making it difficult for him to see the positives along with all the negatives particularly when he hadn't fully grown into his media-God mind-frame'!

DAR DAR: 'If this is all the reality, it's just been a mental battlefield for him his whole life'!

TONY: 'Yeah. He enlightened me at the height of his confusion and becoming unwell, there were things going on in his bedroom (and in his home in general) that the media were aware of including the other media men. He accepts that he is a paranoid schizophrenic but advised me that never at any stage did he feel he was being spied upon. He continued that he was certain his family were not telling the media people anything and he wasn't saying an iota to them either so what else was he supposed to believe other than the fact that somebody living opposite him could see what was going on and those living next door could hear what he was saying and the music he listened to which, to re-iterate, the media were aware of'!

DAR DAR: 'Confusion is the operative word'!

TONY: 'It was at this stage he was thinking that there was a 'battle of media empowerment' going on as he put it. He thought his neighbours were furnishing the media of the actualities as a way of fighting back at empowerment he felt must have been going on through another area of the media'!

DAR DAR: 'As I've just said to you, this is one incredible 'battlefield of the mind' issue and the chap seems to have won it'!

TONY: 'He told me that the media (who unbeknownst to him were all on his side apart from those who were purposely positioned to destroy him) were being infuriated as to how he was being treated so this is why he felt this 'battle of media empowerment' which they were aware of was going on. Although he didn't really know why they were involving themselves because he felt his problems were no different than any other young person's'!

DAR DAR: 'This is unbelievable'!

TONY: 'He said he just didn't know what to think and that people were going off and telling the media of what he was getting up to when he was being social but they have someone or something he sent into the world so that it would be there to serve him when he decided to come to planet earth'!

DAR DAR: 'Fecking mental stuff'!

TONY: 'He says the media have always involved themselves in his life but basically a few things that happened messed up his mind and this relationship (which he is meant to have with broadcasters) was distorted just as he was about to grow into his media-God mind-frame'!

DAR DAR :   'Jesus, Mary and Joseph'!

TONY: 'The way he put it is that it's just unfortunate for him that he happens to have a disorder because of schizophrenia too'!

DAR DAR: 'This bloke's circumstances are very, very unique, ey?'!

TONY: 'I'm telling ya, he has one extremely powerful mind, Dar Dar'!

DAR DAR: 'He certainly does. He's had to contend with so much throughout his life, ey?'!

TONY: 'He says the other media men knew they were inducing him into making mistakes, were acting out total over reaction and blowing things out of proportion. It's been one form of injustice after the next for him throughout his life, he continued'!

DAR DAR: 'He must be an extremely tough person if he's had to deal with all of this abuse particularly via a medium as powerful as television and even more so if he regards it as secular when he's the Spirit'!

TONY: 'Like what you've been realising, 'It's just been one big battlefield for my entire life', he advised'!

DAR DAR: 'It must have been for him indeed'!

TONY: 'He told me that the world has been established and if anyone was have to have exposed it for what it is, he guarantees these men would probably act shocked and also act frightened as if injustices were being done against them when it is they who are the ones who intend to perpetrate the injustices and know what they proponentise is wrong'!

DAR DAR: 'Are you serious?'!

TONY: 'He believes these men know he possesses the intuition and intellect to oppose what has been established, it's the reason he came to planet earth and were doing everything they could to take him out of the equation because they want to assist the creation of the one world system of empty religious doctrine, secular politics, excessive materialism, a lot of games, betting offices and possibly some other things that he has the genius to reject but the average man doesn't'!

DAR DAR: 'Woh'!

TONY: 'He says one should not be embarrassed or ashamed of how they are sexually programmed and shouldn't repress it, let it go defunct nor seek worldly disciplines that would hurt themselves and others. However, he says people of this ilk have an agenda to repress peoples' sexual nature while simultaneously induce transgressions and perversion by being religiously inclined in terms of the evil worldliness of a one world system i.e. the nonsense traditions of our forefathers'!

DAR DAR: 'Oh, right. I think I might understand what he's asserting. A mixture of being a prude and a perv brought about by covering things up, not letting things be fulfilled which would induce people into indulging in illicit sexual practices that would hurt us'!

TONY: 'Yeah. 'The repression of the healthy bringing out the other extreme of being a little sick' is how he put it'!

DAR DAR: 'It could be true alright'!

TONY: 'The media people are out of the way now though'!

DAR DAR: 'You said he regards himself as being a media-God'!

TONY: 'As I informed you the last time, the media know who he is and have been aware that he is the Spirit for his total duration on earth. He is meant to have a relationship with them, he continued'!

DAR DAR: 'There's been things going on alright'!

TONY: 'However, he feels things that are in no way newsworthy were being made so and it's been difficult for him to function let alone properly. He told me he'd be frustrated if they didn't know certain things but it's been the overall package with them at times'!

DAR DAR: 'Did he elaborate?'!

TONY: 'He said that they were embittering him and making him see the negative in most people he was coming into contact with. He knows it's probably not what their intentions were but it's the way it was affecting him and had him feeling so bad about himself'!

DAR DAR: 'Goodness me'!

TONY: 'He told me there is a passage of Scripture where the Spirit refers to his embitterment as he has a feeling this was a Bible passage he inspired because he knew the way the secular media (and secular-ness in general) would induce him into feeling before he came to planet earth'!

DAR DAR: 'It must be very tough on him given his illness too'!

TONY: 'Yeah, I know. They have been involving themselves in a lot of his personal affairs and, because of this, he was vulnerable, unhappy, passive and disturbed. This has been going on all his life and it's because of this that all the negativity and destruction was invited into his life according to him. Although it doesn't help that the world cannot accept him either but at least he might have been better equipped to defend himself had there not been constant media intrusion'!

DAR DAR: 'That's terrible mate'!

TONY: 'However, another reason he remained passive is because he just accepted his fate and knew that because of this he would love his life not so much as to shrink from death at some stage in the future. He didn't want to get in the way of Jesus' and Yahweh's prophecies'!

DAR DAR: 'He's a prophet aswell though'!

TONY: 'His opinion is that the secular media has abused his prophetic and psychic abilities by constantly involving themselves in his personal affairs which only saw to it his fears have been continually realised. There have been all kinds of direct and indirect references relative to the actualities in his life rendering him a repressed prisoner in his very being and circumstances'!

DAR DAR: 'This is far from being the norm'!

TONY: 'He doesn't know which is worse. The fact that he has been caused so many problems by people or the reality of the secular media involving themselves in these issues and reminding him of it all'!

DAR DAR: 'Did he elaborate about any of his mistreatment?'!

TONY: 'He just told me a lot of his problems were during a time when the nature of the relationship he is meant to have with broadcasters was distorted just as he was growing into his media-God mind-frame and just as his psychosis was really beginning to affect him'!

DAR DAR: 'I'm not surprised he has only been surviving and not living like what you told me the last time we talked about him. No wonder the media were getting involved. Although it didn't make things easier with what the other media men knew about him aswell. Those kind of direct references would put a weight on ones' mind'!

TONY: 'He informed me the media have been kind enough to help him with problems and sort out the people who were being cruel and perpetrating injustices against him but he just wants to live for the future now. But, from his viewpoint, their recent involvement in his affairs has been more relative to their own fears than what has been appropriate to his needs'!

DAR DAR: 'I see what you mean. All he wants is his freedom, ey?'!

TONY: 'I'd say that's how he's feeling alright. However, he accepts that the people who were troubling him had to reap what they had sewn and have probably done so with plenty of interest at this stage'!

DAR DAR: 'Yeah, there's been things going on in the media alright. Well, if he is the Counsellor, it's only right they haven't been allowed to get away with having driven him to the brink of suicide, ey?'!

TONY: 'I know. He said it didn't help that he was spiralling with his illness at this time too and it's not their fault that he was unwell. He just wants the exacting of retribution to end in the secular media because it has him reflecting too respectfully on all his issues. He's annoyed with himself for having not stood up for himself better particularly in the work place'!

DAR DAR: 'They drove him to the brink of suicide, didn't they?'!

TONY: 'With all his struggles regarding the media and the non-work-related issues, they did according to him. He was extremely confused'!

DAR DAR: 'He should have told his bosses what was going on if it was non-work-related, ey?'!

TONY: 'Yeah. He should have alright. Some of it was of a sexual nature from both his male and female colleagues too'!

DAR DAR: 'That's awful'!

TONY: ''Because I wasn't doing with my life outside of the work place what they thought I should have been doing they felt they had the right to give me non-work-related harassment inside the work place' he explained'!

DAR DAR: 'Sounds like they were very unprofessional. Well, the world cannot accept him sure it can't?'!

TONY: 'That's what Jesus prophesised in the Gospel of John. Maybe what he said about the more the materially self-sufficient the world and people become, the more it will have difficulty in accepting him and treating him properly is true'!

DAR DAR: 'Mmm. Confusion is a terrible thing. He's obviously a very innocent and pure-minded individual. I've seen him around and he seems to be coping with his issues well enough though'!

TONY: 'He wants to be able to sort his own personal issues out without secular media involvement. However, he says people who feed their materialistic egos tend to be power-players'!

DAR DAR: 'He should be allowed to sort things out for himself without media intrusion alright'!

TONY: 'Once again, he made reference to the fact that we are just about to enter the age of the 'son of perdition'. He revealed that secularists don't want to live out the fundamental but replace and repress their spiritual nature while oppressing with the secular accessories instead and encourage others to do likewise'!

DAR DAR: 'I'm not sure I know what you mean?'!

TONY: 'He says the world has been established and that these secularists are just looking to be empowered into using the things in the world that exist as weapons to hurt people particularly from prophets like him'!

DAR DAR: 'Feck me'!

TONY: 'He says people don't seem to think these worldly things are hurting themselves but they are. He told me secularists are the ultimate sado-masochists who have a very short time to perpetrate pitiful evil knowing they are going into an eternity of suffering'!

DAR DAR: 'I don't know what to say, Tony'!

TONY: 'He accepts all people know is prosperity but he says he is going to have his revenge on secular-ness on planet earth when Yahweh raises him up to be one of His witnesses because of what it did to him as an infant when he knew he would have to deal with it in his future, they trail of destruction it has left in his life particularly his adulthood (and even more so with his struggles with the mental illness), the fact that he has been living in a very, very, very unhappy place because of it and because it has heavily contributed to the reality that some of his future is going to be very disturbing'!

DAR DAR: 'He definitely has psychic abilities alright'!

TONY: 'Getting back to the media, he thinks it might have been a directive from the Lord that the media sort out the power-players who were troubling him'!

DAR DAR: 'Oh, I see'!

TONY: 'He continued that it has been next to impossible for him to refrain from transgressing when he is less aware of what the media know about him than he does himself. He didn't know what were actualities, what were just coincidences and what he was focussing on he was empowering because of his extremely strong spiritual connection'!

DAR DAR: 'It must have been very disturbing for him alright'!

TONY: 'It has been. On top of that, he said the other media men were showing open opposition to the Lord's directive of how the media should treat him and were trying to beat him up into being too nice about things that didn't appeal to him including people, music and so on. He also believes they probably construed he was rebellious and disobedient whenever he was asserting himself which was practically always done in a tough but controlled manner'!

DAR DAR: 'Well, just like everybody else he'd have his preferences and should be allowed to dislike what he wants, ey?'!

TONY: 'In a nut-shell, they were making out that when he was being assertive, he was being disrespectful and blowing things out of proportion in a very purposeful, perpetration-of-injustice way'!

DAR DAR: 'If this is what the reality has always been for him, how has the bloke managed to keep his life going?'!

TONY: 'True. What he said was that if the media refrain from involving themselves in organised, pre-meditated and very purposeful position abuse and not seek to hurt anybody, it doesn't bother him what they know about him. He re-iterated he'd be frustrated if they didn't know certain things because they are meant to be serving him as he is a media-God'!

DAR DAR: 'This is all really powerful mate'!

TONY: 'Another directive the media have probably been given is what they are allowed to use what they know about him over the airwaves. He explained that while he is on planet earth he is part-animal (and not total spirit) and regard must be shown towards his mental, emotional and thus sexual welfare'!

DAR DAR: 'I agree. This bloke's mind is on a completely different level to the average human being mate'!

TONY: 'He says he is aware of the fact that the spirits in Heaven worship Yahweh and when He departs their company, He still lets them know what He's doing. Or something along those lines anyway'!

DAR DAR: 'Yeah. I've heard something about that before'!

TONY: 'He thinks it may have been Yahweh prophesising the way some sections of the media would show no regard for his privacy (and thus his mental, emotional and sexual welfare) which has induced him into making practically all of the mistakes he has and He is relieving him of the extreme guilt He knew he'd suffer from because of this'!

DAR DAR: 'That might very well be true. As he revealed to you, while he is on planet earth he is part animal and regard must be shown for his privacy'!

TONY: 'He's certain the directive Jesus left for what the media should use what they know about him over the airwaves has continually been broken'!

DAR DAR: 'It sounds to me like compensation is something he totally deserves'!

TONY: 'For goodness sake, he's never even known freedom'!

DAR DAR: 'He's wondering why they'll never offer him anything out of their own volition, ey? He should take legal action'!

TONY: 'He doesn't want to do that. They've sorted out a lot of injustices for him. However, 'the son of perdition' has no shortage of weaponry to wound him because he honestly feels the media is something 'the beast' will use to aggravate, antagonise, anger and frustrate him while simultaneously try to deceive people in to thinking he is doing the right thing and show open opposition to everything that is important to him'!

DAR DAR: 'That's probably what will happen'!

TONY: 'Digressing a bit, I was telling you about him feeling one of his books is 'The Little Book' which Yahweh reveres. In this book there is a chapter in which he makes a number of revelations and straightens out a lot of fundamental beliefs. But it is a humorous work throughout. He thinks 'the beast' and 'the false prophet' know about this and (while his publication is comical) they will speak blasphemies in an evil way at his work. 'The beast' will be religiously inclined too but it will be in relation to current false doctrines and worldliness which the ordinary man does not have the genius he has to expose for their emptiness. He's prophesising 'the false prophet' giving 'the beast' his backing and speaking these evil things about GOD in open opposition to his revelations and fundamental beliefs is something that will greatly upset him'!

DAR DAR: 'No wonder he realises some of his future will be distressing'!

TONY: 'Getting back to the media again, he's been through mental and emotional torture but they were probably only doing what they were doing because they are aware of how he's been treated and might feel the power-players who persecuted him during his twenties thought they didn't have to comply with The Golden Rule'!

DAR DAR: 'Yeah, that's what they were doing. They probably just feel a bit sorry for him and sympathise and empathise with his suffering. They were determined to not let them get away with it, ey?'!

TONY: 'True. He said he thinks Jesus foretold 'those people don't care about you'. If He did say this, it may have been in relation to the other media men who were relentlessly trespassing on his life, invading his privacy and violating his very being since he was a baby whom he began to trust just as he was developing into his media-God mind-frame'!

DAR DAR: 'Oh, right'!

TONY: ''What's been done to me my entire life by the secular media can hardly be expressed in words it's so wicked, evil, perverse and diabolical', he continued'!

DAR DAR: 'Well, they're gone now but they can't keep blaming everybody else for their position abuse and the prisoner they've made out of him, can they?'!

TONY: 'That's how he feels alright. He'd much rather they healed up the wounds from the people who broke his heart as opposed to re-opening them. He says it is documented in the back of the Bible about what would go on in his life, how the media should treat him and that he will be able to scream his head off at what he's been put through throughout his life by his persecutors'!

DAR DAR: 'Christ prophesised it all for sure'!

TONY: 'Getting back to the 'they don't care about you' thing, his opinion is that people are aware of what he thinks the Lord might have said and take it personally which has led the various spheres in society into being suspicious that others don't care about them but we should come together and not feel like we have anything to fear from one another as that's what the enemy wants to happen'!

DAR DAR: 'Yeah. It's in relation to him alright but it has been interpreted wrongly in the past with it probably being used to put a strain on the relationship between the various social classes within society. We are going to have to unite when the son of perdition seeks to crush us, ey?'!

TONY: 'I know. He doesn't know whether it was because he was coming down with his psychosis but he can't help get the impression that the love of man grew cold a while back as was prophesised as an indicator that we were entering the last days of the world as we know it'!

DAR DAR: 'Mmm. That's very interesting'!

TONY: 'He told me that hell is a place where those condemned to will feel cold as well as burn. It all depends what you sewed here on earth during your life time'!

DAR DAR: 'You really have to be careful what attitudes you adopt, ey?'!

TONY: 'He says he has his suspicions whom 'the son of perdition' is. He also says he sees the good in everybody because nobody is intrinsically evil (not even 'the beast' and 'the false prophet') but he cannot even bring himself to looking at him without being given the creeps as he believes all that the man is fronting is deception'!

DAR DAR: 'Did he tell you who he is suspicious of?'!

TONY: 'He said he wanted to keep that to himself but to just keep an eye out for who fills that vacant seat number six hundred and sixty six in the European parliament although 'the beast' will set up his office in Jerusalem'!

DAR DAR: 'This is powerful'!

TONY: 'He revealed to me that he himself was born under the star sign of Sagittarius. He says part of being a Sagittarian is that you are a mixture of fire and ice. He was telling me he's certain he has 'extra sensory perception' and that the man he is suspicious of being 'the son of perdition' exudes a deathly warmth and wicked coldness in an evil way because he knows he's the Counsellor and won't accept that he is not God himself. He re-iterated while he is on planet earth he is part-animal and the people conspiring against him were trying to mess him up mentally, emotionally and thus sexually. When he confronts 'the beast' and opposes 'the false prophet', they'll be aware of all his wounds and will most likely try do likewise'!

DAR DAR: 'Are ya serious?'!

TONY: 'He was telling me that he thinks Scripture makes reference to how 'the beast' possesses no needs from women. All that he is interested in are the secular things of the world according to him. Some ministers believe that because he has no needs from women that 'the son of perdition' will be a homosexual but he thinks that it's emotional attachment to females that he lacks. He says he probably has sex with both men and women but there's absolutely no love whatsoever involved'!

DAR DAR: 'Woh'!

TONY: 'He feels 'the beast' could possibly be involved in a marriage of convenience as part of his deception because he will be aware of the fact that the other media men who were conspiring against him were driving wedges between him and relationships with other people (particularly females because they knew he liked the way the feminine mind-set and disposition made him feel as it is compatible with his own masculine ones)'!

DAR DAR: 'That's what he could do alright'!

TONY: 'The other media men were probably making an issue of the fact he wasn't getting involved in a relationship concurrently. He's foretelling 'the son of perdition' might construe that he is not in a marriage of convenience at all. 'How could I possess no needs from females? I am married. It was he who didn't get involved in a relationship with women at all for a long time'. That's the way he imagines 'the beast' might twist things around in terms of he being the good guy and the Counsellor being otherwise as part of his quest to deceive'!

DAR DAR: 'That's what he's foretelling?'!

TONY: 'He also thinks 'the son of perdition' might adopt the attitude that just because he is married (and thus involved in a relationship with a female) that he has the right to be a 'highly-motivated and materialistic control-seeker of worldliness'!

DAR DAR: 'He's sensing 'the son of perdition' is going to be aware of how he was wounded, had his heart broke and was driven to the brink of suicide, ey?'!

TONY: 'That's what he's prophesising'!

DAR DAR: 'This isn't good'!

TONY: 'As I told you before, he told me he was frightened of having sex with a girl for just out of lust and the only way he felt he would get one hundred per cent pure spiritual love is if Yahweh gave this to him and that's what he requested from God back during the Summer of 1992'!

DAR DAR: 'I don't know what to say'!

TONY: 'With all the problems he had had with the media he was side-tracked and de-secured from realising he is His Spirit'!

DAR DAR: 'Yeah, I remember you telling me that'!

TONY: 'As I said to you the last time, he's had erectile dysfunction since 1992 and has really struggled with his mental health welfare over the last twenty years too which disenabled him from entering a relationship. His disorder would have made having sex a great difficulty in addition. Not getting the necessary communication from a previous friendship made it hard to move on aswell. He told me he has had a number of opportunities to get this closure but he was either unaware or totally confused when his empathisers approached him'!

DAR DAR: 'Oh, right'!

TONY: 'He said the media have been dealing with the people who were troubling him, they had to reap what they had sewn and it was only right they were pulled up for driving him to the brink of taking his own life. However, it has had him totally confused (as he just doesn't understand certain things) and he was very disturbed when people were trying to help him out communication-wise'!

DAR DAR: 'He's just very innocent and pure-minded'!

TONY: 'He says 'the beast' will be aware of the fact that he played games aswell. He wanted to stop playing football at the age of ten because he just wished to be friends with his dad and the other media men were inducing him into being a power-player'!

DAR DAR: 'It's part of their plans that they induce people into being power-players according to him, isn't it?'!

TONY: 'That's what he believes'!

DAR DAR: 'I'm beginning to sense he's right regarding this issue'!

TONY: 'He continued that he attained a soccer scholarship to University College, Dublin back in 1990 but these men did everything they could to mess up his career and induced him into making mistakes when he became a public figure. He's certain that when he was forced out of his scholarship by a few people and walked away from semi-professional football (because he saw through the emptiness of the game and the football world in general), they probably made a big fuss of it despite mentally, emotionally and thus sexually abusing him in the interim'!

DAR DAR: 'You did tell me before that they were putting up a front of being on his side but were abusing him constantly outside of what they were fronting. It's was all abuse, lies and deception with them, ey?'!

TONY: 'It probably was alright'!

DAR DAR: 'Did he elaborate on what he means by the emptiness of the football world?'!

TONY: 'He said he didn't enjoy being paid to play and all the big egos in the dressing room. He also told me it became apparent to him that he could be sold on to a bigger club and didn't want to feel like a piece of meat and had too much respect for himself to be used as a 'product of trade' as he put it. He felt there was so much more to living life than being a professional footballer'!

DAR DAR: 'I don't know what to say'!

TONY: 'He went on that during a game he reacted to some provocation the wrong way and when he walked off the pitch he said to himself 'it's either be a good footballer or be a good Christian because you cannot be both'. He decided being the best Christian he could be was so much more important'!

DAR DAR: 'Is that what he said to himself?'!

TONY: 'He deduced that playing games brought out everything in humans i.e. being an instrument of the Lord but also being an instrument of control and thus sin and death'!

DAR DAR: 'This bloke is unbelievable'!

TONY: ''I find adulation from power-players a very difficult thing to deal with', he confessed. 'That's another reason why I walked away from semi-professional football', he added!

DAR DAR: 'He's obviously very humble'!

TONY: 'He continued another thing 'the son of perdition' will know is that he worked in the financial world for a few years which was all to his own aggravation (because he's not designed for that kind of work) but he has an honours bachelor of arts degree in economics and a master's degree in economic science which he went on to earn in university that he felt he should make the most of'!

DAR DAR: 'It seems to me he feels like he's done a few things with his life which only ended up making him unhappy but what the other media men were doing to him was putting a weight on his mind and was disenabling him from making proper judgements. He was only doing what they were inducing him into doing because they wanted to hurt him and wished for him to do things with his life that would make him unhappy, ey?'!

TONY: 'That's exactly what he realises alright'!

TONY: 'He went on that he loves and cares for those who have hassled him but it has been a very negative experience. He said that he'd hoped he'd make lots of friends for life but has so little to show for all his 'investments of love'. He said he ended up with a lot of enemies who in turn created enemies for him. He continued it's just all very unfortunate and he accepts he is the most misunderstood entity in the Bible so what would mere mortals know?'!

DAR DAR: 'I have to say I think I'd feel something similar if I had to live with the fact that I was driven to the brink of suicide'!

TONY: 'He told me he accepts that from their viewpoint they probably felt they could only allow themselves to be subject to so much discipline but it's heart-breaking for him as it was all very empty in his opinion'!

DAR DAR: 'Yeah, I know what you mean'!

TONY: 'He insisted one cannot be expected to reflect positively when so much negativity has been sewn'!

DAR DAR: 'You'd have to respect his viewpoint'!

TONY: ''People were adopting an attitude that I was only deserving of being treated properly if they were getting what they wanted out of me or if I was doing with my life what they thought I should be', he explained'!

DAR DAR: 'He's the Counsellor and yet he was being dictated to like this. It's a serious issue that the Spirit of the Sovereign Lord was subjected to this kind of attitude, ey?'!

TONY: 'It most certainly is. He continued that they didn't have to appreciate it if they didn't want but it is his life afterall and he knows the way they treated him is a serious issue given that he is the Spirit of their Supernatural Father and Creator of the Universe'!

DAR DAR: 'They better learn how to apologise profusely to him'!

TONY: 'They better alright but it won't be his wishes that they perish, he re-assured. They just didn't know who it was they were dealing with, his psychosis and all his struggles with the media throughout his life'!

DAR DAR: 'Well, if he's always had to contend with the media too, I understand that things must have been very difficult for him'!

TONY: 'He argued that getting involved with someone is something you have to feel comfortable about doing. It shouldn't be dictated to the individual'!

DAR DAR: 'He's right'!

TONY: ''It was as if I wasn't even entitled to quality of life on my own terms when it came to them although they probably felt like I was indulging in pride of life in fairness', he continued. 'However, I like people who give you the benefit of the doubt', he asserted'!

DAR DAR: 'The poor guy'!

TONY: ''However, there's their side of the story too' he continued'!

DAR DAR: 'Well, that's true. Maybe they should have tried to see things from his viewpoint. And, as he said, people should give you the benefit of the doubt as he'd not purposely trouble anyone because he's just a bit on the quiet side, ey?'!

TONY: ''You have to live and let live' he said'!

DAR DAR: 'I couldn't agree more'!

TONY: 'I know. He said he was made famous before he was really ready to be so, it was on other peoples' terms and it included being so for reasons he didn't want to be. It probably wouldn't have been a problem but the other media men were trying to ruin everything for him concurrently. He also told me that for a decade or more he wasn't even aware of his own circumstances because, to re-cap, the nature of the relationship he is meant to have with media people was distorted just as he was developing into the media-God he has become'!

DAR DAR: 'I don't know what to say'!

TONY: 'He told me another thing the other media
               men were doing was trying to destroy his life
               memories while preventing him from learning
               from life as he went along. To repeat, they were
               relentlessly trespassing upon his life, invading
               his privacy and violating his very being. They
               were also driving wedges between him and
               relationships with others while simultaneously
               ridiculing those he cared for to most likely
               make him seek loneliness to avoid the abuse.
               They were perversifying his character and
               circumstances and he is certain fuelling peoples'
               negative opinions and attitudes towards him in
               order to induce others into giving him unfair
               attention in addition. They were misrepresenting
               him and misconstruing also. It's a miracle he's
               still alive'!

DAR DAR: 'If this is true he must have been through mental
               and emotional torture for sure'!

TONY: 'He thinks it would be difficult to have ever
               encountered a more confused individual who has
               lived on earth'!

DAR DAR: 'It doesn't even bear thinking about what he's
               been through throughout his time here but
               does he not accept that a lot of it is imaginary
               because he has a disorder due to his illness, ey?'!

TONY: 'I actually asked him that and he accepts he
               is a paranoid schizophrenic but he insisted
               it happened far too often for it to be just
               coincidence or symptomatic of schizophrenia.
               They were definitely direct and indirect actuality
               immersements making him a repressed prisoner
               in his very being and circumstances. He told me
               that even when he had a psychotic episode the

psychiatrist advised him there is nothing wrong with his cognitive ability'!

DAR DAR: 'I really don't know what to say'!

TONY: 'He continued that for the rest of his lifetime he is going to have to live with the fact that but for his faith in Jesus Christ (and the reality that he felt he would go to hell for the rest of eternity if he did commit suicide) he probably would have ended it all. And even then there was an upwards of ninety per cent chance that he was going to do it anyway'!

DAR DAR: 'I don't know what to say'!

TONY: 'He also says the angel (whom he's been waiting to be friends with) he encountered out in Tamangos (a night club on Dublin's north side) gave him something very special to remain alive for too'!

DAR DAR: 'I hope he gets his wish to become friends with her'!

TONY: ''She was an instrument of interest, positivity and such life during what was a very dark and confusing time period for me', he added. 'She definitely has a key to my heart and since she chatted me up, she has never left my feelings', he said. 'To see her with another man would destroy me', he continued'!

DAR DAR: 'Sounds like he's spent a long time investing hope they'll be friends'!

TONY: 'He has been praying to Jesus constantly that he and she become part of one anothers' lives'!

DAR DAR: 'She probably thinks he's really cute too but he just doesn't realise it. The poor bloke, it probably means so much to him he's totally insecure'!

TONY: 'He said he gets weak at the thoughts of being in her company. When he encountered her all those years ago, his head got light, his heart started thumping, there were butterflies in his stomach and his knees buckled'!

DAR DAR: 'He's a deeply sensitive individual, ey?'!

TONY: 'He is. I hope so much they become close friends aswell'!

DAR DAR: 'After all he's been through, he deserves at least some happiness'!

TONY: 'Getting back to things a bit, he continued that coupled with schizophrenia there is a huge guilt factor he's dealing with. He knows he shouldn't reflect upon things the way he does but he's been made to feel like a right b*stard when he admitted that he is a deeply sensitive individual although he knows he's tough. He is suffering because of all the secular-ness'!

DAR DAR: 'That's very sad'!

TONY: 'He just said humiliation (particularly of a sexual nature) followed by secular-ness induces people into exacting retribution'!

DAR DAR: 'I understand'!

TONY: 'Apparently Jesus said during His Sermon on the Mount that you cannot serve money and serve

God. However, finance is a necessary evil but if it does exist, then it should be governed by the proper principles'!

DAR DAR: 'I didn't know that'!

TONY: 'In his opinion, unless the business world refrains from being motivated by fear and greed, materialistic usurpers will continue to cause so much inequality and tribulation'!

DAR DAR: 'The guy is just fretting over having nothing to show for his 'investments of love' alright'!

TONY: 'Well, he does know he is going to hate his life at some stage in the future. He says maybe those who hurt him will try to heal his wounds but the damage has been done which is unfortunate because all people know is prosperity'!

DAR DAR: 'This is terrible. There's been an absolute trail of destruction left in his life by the media and the people he's come into contact with, he's suffering because of the cruel nature of his illness and now at least some of his future is going to be very painful. He's just always been, is and always will be a prisoner to unfortunate circumstances'!

TONY: 'I know. He continued that these people have probably had their feelings hurt at some stage during their lives too and the way human beings can treat one another at times is so sad'!

DAR DAR: 'I think I'm going to start to cry'!

TONY: 'I was close to it earlier when he was explaining everything to me too'!

DAR DAR: 'I don't think I want to hear much more. It's upsetting stuff'!

TONY: 'He finished that he feels sad because it is written in Scripture that the world will rejoice and make merry when he is martyred along with the other witness on the streets of Jerusalem and reject their advice that the inhabitants of the planet should come to repentance for all that has been proponentised'!

DAR DAR: 'The story of his life is a heartbreaking one'!

TONY: 'To re-iterate, the 'son of perdition' is going to proponentise peace and prosperity shortly but once he and the other witness are resurrected, people will realise that feeding your materialistic ego damages spirituality. They'll realise it's all superficial nonsense in many respects. People will learn that he lived a very simple and humble lifestyle and will want to imitate him because he's the Counsellor. This reality and the fact that people won't want to be pawns of consumerism to sustain the material and the lack of demand for materialism thereafter might contribute to the markets getting into trouble. The way he put it is that the 'control-seekers of worldliness elitists' are dictating to genuine servants and people probably won't want to be subject to their power vacuum'!

DAR DAR: 'That's revelation to me mate'!

TONY: 'He continued that the markets will have to stay afloat so it's going to highly inflate the natural things on earth like metals, crops, oil and so on. Water is the most plentiful substance on earth but even that will become valuable when

Wormwood (which he is claiming to have seen in a vision from the future which was shown to him while asleep several years ago) poisons a third of the planet's supply as foretold in the Book of Revelations, he's prophesising'!

DAR DAR: 'We really are in the very last days alright mate'!

TONY: 'He told me the huge guilt factor within those here on earth in the period after his resurrection (because the majority of the world will reject him and then learn who he really is and what he's been through his whole life) could be something 'the beast' plays on to turn everybody against one another but he hopes his resurrection will at least bring the world to accepting Jesus Christ as Lord and Saviour. Although it is going to be very difficult to preach the Gospel thereafter. However, Yahweh is in control of everything and will enable it somehow with supernatural assistance'!

DAR DAR: 'That's beginning to make a little bit of sense mate. Everybody will probably be blaming everyone else'!

TONY: 'He doesn't drink, smoke, gamble, do drugs or eat pig meat. He detests a non-fundamentally regulated financial world (and the explosion of finance in general), bad business principles, empty religious doctrine, secular politics, materialistic greed, the current world order, a lot of games and betting offices'!

DAR DAR: 'He lives a very humble and pure lifestyle. If he's rejected by people, they are going to be here on earth and experience the 'wrath of the Almighty', right?'!

TONY: 'He said planet earth could be a very frightening place to be when all the 'finger of fudgements' are being cast as he put it'!

DAR DAR: 'People can think what they want about him but the chap is a genius, Tony'!

TONY: 'He's a prophetic and psychic genius too mate'!

DAR DAR: 'That he is too for sure'!

TONY: 'Before I go, he says he's heard other things at Mass which he is certain Jesus Christ prophesised which go something along the lines of 'your family and friends will turn their backs on you, you'll be rejected by kings and you'll be sent to prison'. He honestly believes the media men are going to reap into their own lives what they have always sought to sew into his. 'Although wouldn't it be gas if it was in relation to 'the son of perdition'', he joked! Like I told you a while ago, they were driving wedges between him and relationships with all of those he loved. He says they were basically trying to turn him into a paranoid and deluded loner while simultaneously inviting negative attention into his life by inducing him into making mistakes and then perversifying his character and circumstances'!

DAR DAR: 'Yeah, I've heard that at Mass alright. Goodness me, people have always thought it would be in relation to them if they were to stay loyal to their Christianity in latter days but maybe it's not at all, is it?'!

TONY: 'I'm sensing it's in relation to those media men who were abusing him. He continued that the incorrect interpretation has resulted in peoples' fear levels being heightened which would only turn us against one another as we'd want to protect our own individual feelings and would see us unnecessarily regard others as enemies when they are our spiritual siblings, right?'!

DAR DAR: 'That's what he realises and wants others to realise also. I'm telling ya, it's the fecking truth mate'!

TONY: 'It definitely is alright'!

DAR DAR: 'They really were doing everything they could to take him out of the equation'!

TONY: 'They were. It's a no-brainer'!

DAR DAR: 'Yeah. What he's saying is true'!

TONY: 'He said defiantly 'it is mission well and truly unaccomplished from their viewpoint''!

DAR DAR: 'Fair bleedin' balls to him. Legend and a half the bloke is'!

TONY: 'He told me you have to remain the person that became the person in the first place. He doesn't want to be known for much else outside of his spirituality and sense of humour'!

DAR DAR: 'A gentleman and a scholar is what he is. I've nothing but admiration for him'!

TONY: 'Finally. He informed me that the same gentleman who was a guest on 'Extreme Prophetic' was on another programme on The GOD Channel called 'It's Supernatural' only a few months ago and he was saying Jesus

Christ showed him a vision of a dove (signifying the Spirit) being set free from a cage (i.e. imprisonment). For the first time in his life he is beginning to experience freedom from the secular media'!

DAR DAR: 'So what he was telling you about never being anything other than a prisoner because of these losers who were positioned in the media and the good media people who had to ensure the people who treated him the way they did had to reap what they had sewn is obviously true'!

TONY: 'This bloke's class! I'll call into you again if he reveals anything else to me'!

DAR DAR: 'He is. Please do let me know if he has more to say. See you later'!

TONY: 'Look after yourself'!